D0846666

SOCCER

PLAY·THE·GAME

SOCCER

Ken Goldman & Peter Dunk ·

Ward Lock Limited · London

© Ward Lock Limited 1988
© Illustrations Ward Lock Limited 1988

First published in Great Britain in 1988
by Ward Lock Limited, 8 Clifford Street,
London W1X 1RB, an Egmont Company

All Rights Reserved. No part of this publication
may be reproduced, stored in a retrieval system,
or transmitted, in any form or by any means,
electronic, mechanical, photocopying, recording,
or otherwise, without the prior permission of the
Copyright owners.

Series Editor Ian Morrison
Designed by Anita Ruddell
Illustrated by Bob Williams
Diagrams by Ian Foulis

Text set in Helvetica
by Hourds Typographica, Stafford, England
Printed and bound in Great Britain
by Richard Clay Ltd, Bungay, Suffolk

British Library Cataloguing in Publication Data
Goldman, Ken
    Play the game : soccer.
    1. Association football. Manuals
    I. Title   II. Dunk, Peter
    796.334'2

    ISBN 0-7063-6665-4

Acknowledgments

The authors and publishers would like to
thank Colorsport for supplying the
photographs reproduced in this book.

**Frontispiece: A confetti-spotted Diego
Maradona, captain of Argentina and one of
the game's greatest players, triumphantly
embraces the World Cup, Mexico 1986.**

CONTENTS

FOREWORD

It is with great pleasure that I write this foreword for a publication which I consider will be of tremendous interest to the football enthusiast.

Much is made of the coaching field in modern times, and it is clearly noticeable that there are many conflicting views and thoughts on how football should be played. Often we tend to move away from the simplicity of the game into an area which can create some confusion for the participating players. However, this new book, *Play the Game: Soccer,* retains that important simplicity whilst at the same time fully explaining all the more complex aspects of football for both the player and the coach.

I personally welcome the inclusion of such subjects as terminology and rules, as these are areas which tend to be overused or understated, whichever suits. How often we hear coaches using phrases which may be inappropriate and confusing to the players; how often we criticize the match officials when we are unaware of the laws of the game. The references in this book are there to be read and used for confirmation of our thoughts and ideas. Discipline and basic commonsense play a vital part in our football lives, and it is important to remember the coach needs to know how to impart his beliefs and discipline in a correct and imposing manner, and the player needs to know how to respond in the right way.

Play the Game: Soccer offers so much to both the player and the coach, adding to their knowledge and stimulating them both into being better and achieving more.

John Lyall
Manager of West Ham United FC

FOREWORD

It's a fact: youngsters today don't spend as much time playing with a football as they used to in days gone by. As well as greater academic demands, from homework to passing exams, they also have a greater variety of sports and leisure activities to choose from, ranging from snooker and tennis to home computers.

This being the case, a short cut to learning and understanding football skills needs to be made available. The modern young footballer needs swift coaching and organizing: he wants to know the how, when, where and why and the best way of playing good football, as quickly and effectively as possible. Youth team managers and coaches want to know that they are teaching the correct techniques and improving the skills and knowledge of the youngsters they are looking after. In other words, that they are doing the job correctly.

This book is just what the doctor ordered. The techniques are well-diagrammed, the rules are clearly explained, and the history of the game concisely written. All in all, *Play the Game: Soccer* is an extremely useful book.

Don Howe
England national team coach

HISTORY &
DEVELOPMENT OF
SOCCER

It is impossible to say where, or by whom, football was invented. Certainly the ancient Greeks included a ball in some of their military training exercises, and it seems that this idea was adopted and adapted by the Romans, who spread it throughout their empire. Perhaps in this way the game first arrived on Britain's shores. But there is also evidence that some form of game involving kicking or carrying a ball into your opponents' territory was played in ancient times by the Chinese, the Egyptians and the Assyrians.

The principle of the game has always been the same – a conflict in which two teams try to force a ball to their opponents' base by kicking, throwing or carrying, and this principle applies to all forms of modern football – Association, Rugby, American, Gaelic, Australian Rules and others.

Although the Romans may have introduced the game to Britain, there is no evidence of the game's widespread popularity in these islands until the time of the Norman conquest in the eleventh century. By the time of William the Conqueror's death, the game had taken root right across the social spectrum, from aristocrat to peasant, but no clear and uniform rules were to be defined for a further 600 years and the game developed very slowly, if at all.

It was certainly a hard game in those days. There are two documented incidents, in 1280 and 1325, of footballers dying after falling on their daggers, and the only sorts of rules which did apply to the game were those which sought to abolish it. Edward III, Richard II and Henry IV, all worried by the military threat from France, each banned football on the grounds that it was not ideal military training and interfered with the much more valuable archery practice.

None of these bans had any lasting effect. The game survived in its various forms throughout the British Isles, and by the beginning of the nineteenth century, although there were still no rules, the game had at least taken on a shape that would probably be recognized by modern-day crowds as a sort of cross between soccer and rugby.

Stanley Matthews, an inspiration to generations of footballers, in his days at Blackpool.

It was at about this time, in the early years of the nineteenth century, that there was a fairly rapid proliferation in education for the privileged few. The public schools started to appear, and attracted pupils both from the aristocracy and the new money of the industrial revolution. There was neither the time nor the facilities in most of these schools for the pupils to pursue the sports popular around the country houses of the day, such as riding, fishing, hunting or horse racing, but it was a simple matter to take up a village game like football. All you needed were two teams and a ball, and a convenient field or yard on the school campus.

Football – essentially a simple but thrilling game – soon became very popular in public schools. And in one such school – Rugby – the educationalist Dr Thomas Arnold started to take notice. Personally, he was not much interested in sport, but he could see that his boys were obsessed with it. Arnold was a man who liked to instil discipline and a sense of purpose into his students, and he therefore set about applying these principles to football.

Other schools soon followed suit by organizing their own football rules, and in hardly any time at all the game was the major sports activity at public schools throughout the land. But each school had its own rules, and there was no competition between schools, so the game continued to develop in a rather haphazard way, some forms of which, such as the Eton Wall Game, survive to this day.

Meanwhile, back at Rugby School in the early 1800s, one of the rules was that handling was only allowed for a fair catch, and running with the ball in your hands was forbidden. Then, one afternoon in 1823 a pupil from Manchester called William Webb Ellis, who later became a clergyman, caught the ball and ran with it tucked under his arm to the opponents' goal line. This caused some debate at the school, and not long afterwards 'running in' became an accepted part of Rugby's football. It remains to this day as the principal distinction between rugby and soccer.

As the boys from the public school went up to university, however, it proved difficult to organize games because all the players in the pool came from different schools where different rules applied. Often, matches were preceded by a considerable amount of correspondence in which the rules for that particular match were ironed out. Basic questions such as how big the pitch should be, how many players should be on each side, and would carrying the ball be permitted had to be sorted out afresh on virtually every occasion, and it became clearer as time went by that a uniform code was needed.

Gradually, boys from Rugby School, together with others who preferred the Rugby game, tended to play only amongst themselves, while boys from other schools, notably Charterhouse and Westminster, concentrated on the so-called 'dribbling game'. And it seems from what evidence is available that this dribbling game was not much fun as a spectacle. The idea was not to pass the ball around among your team-mates, building an offensive move or getting out of dangerous situations near your own goal, but rather for whoever had possession at any given moment to attempt to dribble his way through virtually the entire opposing team, who would gang up in a tight mob to stop him.

This sort of scrimmaging is still part of rugby's code, but it must have produced the most dour of interminable midfield struggles in early nineteenth-century soccer, and often there were no goals, even though as many as three consecutive afternoons would be put aside for a single game.

Then, in 1848, a seven-hour meeting took place at Cambridge University between fourteen men from a variety of public schools, and this marathon session produced the 'Cambridge Rules' which were widely adopted and modified twice during the next decade. The Cambridge Rules give us a fascinating insight into what football was like in those years, particularly as only a few scraps of the individual school rules in force prior to 1848 have survived.

Under the Cambridge Rules, goals were awarded for balls kicked between the goal posts and under a string; goal kicks and throw-ins were given as today, except that throw-ins were one-handed and could consequently travel further; catching the ball on the full from a kick was allowed, although running with the ball to hand was forbidden; and for the first time an offside rule which we would recognize today was established. Prior to 1848, anybody in front of the ball was in an offside position, but the new rules allowed that you could receive a pass from behind providing that there were at least three defenders goalside of you.

With an accepted code now in force, inter-school and inter-university football flourished in the 1850s, and some time around 1855 the first known football club was formed in Sheffield. An offshoot of the Sheffield Cricket Club, which had just moved into new premises at Bramall Lane, it was called simply Sheffield Football Club and had its own constitution and set of rules, based on the Cambridge Rules. Within five years there were no fewer than fifteen clubs in and around Sheffield and it is recorded that in 1861 arch-rivals Sheffield and Hallam played to a gate of 600 spectators.

But there were still endless discussions going on about the rules, and back at Cambridge modified rules were published in November 1862 (the same year that the oldest Football League club, Notts County, came into being) and these became the basis for the Laws of the Football Association, which was founded in the following year.

By 1863, football was still a rather different game from the one we know today. Handling the ball was still allowed, and a player who caught the ball cleanly could make a mark and so win a free kick. There was even a touch-down rule, allowing for a free kick at

goal in the event of the ball being touched down by an attacker behind his opponents' goal line. But within the space of a few years, the 'rugby' elements of Association Football had been abandoned, and the game has remained basically the same ever since.

Indeed, when the Football Association was formed, acrimonious arguments between the followers of rugby and soccer became so ill-tempered that the resulting split between supporters of the two codes proved too wide ever to repair. Interestingly, the main bone of contention was not the question of running with the ball, but that of so-called 'hacking'. Rugby men thought it perfectly acceptable to tackle an opponent by kicking him on the shin, and when soccer's supporters voted this out, the rugby followers accused them of cowardice and walked out of the FA, never to return.

And so we come to the most important date in the history of football – Monday 26 October, 1863. On that day, in the Freemasons' Tavern in Great Queen Street in London's Lincoln's Inn Fields, a meeting was held. On the following day, *The Times* carried this story:

■ FOOTBALL – Last evening a meeting of the captains or other representatives of the football clubs of the metropolis was held at the Freemason's Tavern, Great Queen-street, Lincoln's Inn-Fields. Mr. Pember, N.N. Kilburn Club, having been voted to the chair, observed that the adoption of a certain set of rules by all football players was greatly to be desired, and said that the meeting had been called to carry that object into effect as far as practicable. Mr. E.C. Morley (Barnes) moved, and Mr. Mackenzie (Forest Club, Leytonstone) seconded, the following resolution: 'That it is advisable that a football association should be formed for the purpose of settling a code of rules for the regulation of the game of football.'

The resolution was eventually passed despite the intervention of Charterhouse School, whose representative felt he could not pledge himself to such a course of action until other public schools had been canvassed for their opinion.

Surprisingly, there were no representatives from Cambridge at the meeting, although they had been the first ones to attempt to codify the rules, and as a consequence the thirteen rules which eventually emerged reflected the men who were involved in the FA at its birth. They were mostly old Harrovians, and their rules were essentially those in operation at the famous Harrow school at the time. The strange 'N.N. Kilburn Club' mentioned in *The Times* was the No Names Kilburn Club, consisting of old Harrovians, and another club made up of former Harrow pupils was Forest School, which later became the famous Wanderers.

Mr Campbell of Blackheath, who had been elected as the first Treasurer of the fledgling FA, did not last long. By the end of the year, Blackheath had broken away, preferring to stick to the Rugby code, and indeed the FA made no real attempt in its early years to tackle the problems of codifying the rules on a national basis. It was not until Charles Alcock, another old Harrovian, became secretary that things began to move. In 1867 representatives from Yorkshire (home of the oldest club – Sheffield, joined the FA and by 1870 representative matches were taking place between unofficial England and Scotland sides and others.

Then, in 1871, Alcock made the historic suggestion that the FA should establish a challenge cup competition 'for which all clubs belonging to the Football Association should be invited to compete'. There were fifteen entries in the first year, although only twelve teams actually took part.

The incomparable Pele – perhaps the greatest footballer of all time.

The Wanderers, captained by Charles Alcock himself, went on to win the first FA Cup final by beating the Royal Engineers 1-0, at the Oval, and 2000 people paid what was then a fairly expensive one shilling each for the privilege of watching.

1872 was also the year which marked the first official international between England and Scotland. This was another brainchild of Alcock's. The match resulted in a goalless draw – a scoreline not repeated in England v Scotland matches for the next ninety-eight years – and the English were, to put it mildly, rather surprised by a Scottish team selected entirely from the ranks of Queen's Park. Perhaps what had surprised them most was the fact that the Scots did not play the 'dribbling' game which typified English football. English public schoolboys had been encouraged to demonstrate their individual brilliance by simply running at the opposition until they had lost the ball, and English teams usually played with a goalkeeper, two defenders and as many as eight dribbling forwards. The canny Scots had, however, worked out that passing the ball was a much more effective way of making progress upfield. English players themselves soon adopted the passing game.

By 1877 football was taking on a shape which would be recognizable today. By that year the FA rules were generally accepted throughout the country, free kicks and throw-ins (both innovations of the Sheffield club) were adopted, the crossbar, first used two years earlier, was brought into general use, the game was limited to ninety minutes' duration, handling the ball was restricted to the goalkeeper and neutral referees were required.

Within a decade the FA, guided by Charles Alcock, accepted professionalism and in 1885 James Forrest of Blackburn Rovers became the first professional to play for England. His fee was ten shillings per match. This new professionalism spread rapidly in the north of England, but not so in the south, and inevitably the northern clubs started to dominate.

On 2 March 1888, William McGregor, a director of Aston Villa, wrote to other clubs urging the necessity for the major clubs to establish a definite list of fixtures. Gates for matches other than FA Cup ties had been falling, and such fixtures as were arranged were subject to cancellation either because the opponents failed to turn up, or because cup replays had to be played on dates which had already been booked. McGregor felt that the guarantee of the match actually taking place, plus the added attraction of competitive football, would bring back the crowds, and of course he was right.

The first meeting took place on Friday 23 March 1888 at Anderton's Hotel in London on the eve of the FA Cup final. Less than a month later – on 17 April – matters were finalized at the Royal Hotel in Manchester. No southern clubs were involved, and as it was decided that no more than twenty-two dates could be made available for League games, only twelve clubs were enlisted as members. And so the Football League, the world's oldest League, was formed.

Preston were the first champions, winning the title without losing a game and lifting the FA Cup in the same season without conceding a goal, but Aston Villa were the real stars of the pre-First World War era, winning the League six times and the FA Cup five times in that period. The northern and midland clubs enjoyed total domination of football prior to 1914. In 1892 the League absorbed the rival Football Alliance and expanded to a membership of twenty-eight clubs in two divisions, none from south of Birmingham. A year later Arsenal were elected to the Second Division.

Soon after the First World War, in 1920, the Southern League was swallowed up to form the Third Division, and a year later a northern section of twenty clubs was added. This was increased to the twenty-two in 1923, and so with eighty-eight clubs in four divisions the League had grown into a structure which has remained virtually unchanged ever since, with two more clubs being elected to each of the Third Division sections in 1950 to bring it up to its present strength of ninety-two.

While football was going from strength to strength in the homeland of the modern game, similar interest was being shown overseas. Probably the oldest association to be formed outside the British Isles was Denmark's **Boldspil Union**, established as early as 1889, and by the turn of the century football associations had sprung up in many other countries. In those days they all looked to Britain for leadership, but British football displayed an almost incredible insularity and it would not be until 1946 that the British associations finally settled down to permanent membership of FIFA, world football's governing body.

Several attempts were made by overseas associations to involve the British in the formation of an international body, but all were rejected. Delegates from various other European countries went to Paris on 21 May 1904 and the **Fédération Internationale de Football Association** (FIFA) was formed. The founder members were Belgium, Denmark, France, Netherlands, Spain, Sweden and Switzerland. Two years later, the British associations belatedly realized the extent to which soccer was flourishing on the continent and relented. Amazingly, despite their arrogance, the British were still held in high regard, and D.B. Woolfall of the English FA was elected President of FIFA in 1906, remaining in office until his death in 1918.

Then the trouble started. The British associations refused to play against countries which had fought against them during the war, and left FIFA. Six years later, in 1924, they re-affiliated but promptly started an argument about the definition of amateurism. The payment of hotel and travelling expenses to amateur players was acceptable to the British, but they could not accept the view taken by most Europeans that it was also reasonable to compensate players for any loss of earnings involved in representing their country. When these 'broken time' payments were allowed in the 1928 Olympics, it was too much for the British, and they withdrew from the Olympic movement and FIFA, not rejoining the latter body until after the Second World War.

But the remaining members of FIFA were determined to get the World Cup underway with or without the British, and so they did, in 1930. A year earlier, FIFA had met in Barcelona with a view to organizing the first tournament, and there were five candidates for the position of host nation – Spain, Netherlands, Italy, Sweden and Uruguay. When the Uruguayans made the astonishing offer of paying the travelling and accommodation expenses for all the visiting teams, and building a new stadium (the Centenary Stadium) for the event, the four European candidates, realizing that they could not possibly match such an offer, withdrew from the competition in a huff, but the World Cup went ahead in Uruguay in 1930 and the greatest tournament in world football was begun.

In the years since 1930 football has remained virtually the same game that we know today, although the laws have been tinkered with. Perhaps the most significant change had already taken place, for in the summer of 1925 the offside law was changed so that the 'fewer than three defenders between the attacker and the goal' was altered to read 'fewer than two'. This had become necessary because many teams were employing offside traps that were so effective that play was more or less confined to the middle of the field. The effect of the change was dramatic. In the following season almost fifty per cent more goals were scored in League matches.

The most significant post-war developments have probably been in the proliferation of football to a truly global scale, helped in no small measure by the growth of international competition at club and national level – and by television. The World Cup was already underway, but has now reached the point where it is one of the largest spectator events in the world. Then, in the mid-1950s European club football was started, followed within a few years by the European Nations' Cup (now the European Championship). The English League Cup started in 1960, and equivalent domestic league and cup competitions now exist in nearly all countries which play soccer on an organized basis.

Most boys (and more and more girls!) kick a football from the moment they start walking. For those who show that extra bit of talent there are plenty of coaches available to develop that ability. If you are such a player, don't be afraid to go for extra coaching. Remember, the likes of Bryan Robson, Peter Shilton and Glen Hoddle are still learning all the time.

EQUIPMENT & TERMINOLOGY

The pitch

The playing surface can be either grass or an artificial surface. The field of play shall be rectangular and measure between 100–130yd (90–120m) in length and 50–100yd (45–90m) wide. We can see you saying already; 'Well, if the minimum length is 100 yards and the maximum width is 100 yards then the pitch can be square' . . . wrong. The rules clearly state it cannot be square because the length *must exceed the width*.

The boundary lines down the 'long' side of the pitch are called touch-lines and those across the width of the pitch at each end are goal-lines. All boundary lines and other pitch markings are 5in (0.12m) wide and form part of the field of play.

The other pitch markings are:

A centre line is drawn across the pitch at a point mid-way between the two touch-lines. At the middle of the centre-line is a centre-spot, where all kick-offs start from. A circle with a 10yd (9.15m) radius is drawn from the centre-spot. This creates the centre circle. At each corner of the field of play are four corner flags, each a minimum of 5ft (1.5m) high. They are positioned at a point where the goal-lines and touch-lines meet. A quadrant with a 1yd (1m) radius is drawn at each corner of the field. You will often see flags along the middle of the touch-lines. But these are optional.

At the centre of each goal-line is situated a goal. Two lines are drawn at right-angles to the goal line 6yd (5.5m) from the

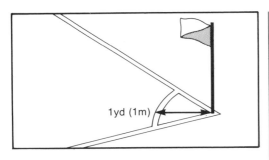

The corner flag.

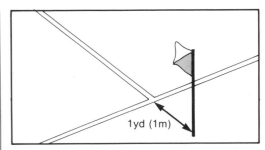

The halfway flag.

1yd (1m)

The field of play.

'Minimum of 3yd (3m) advised between boundaries of field and spectator enclosure'

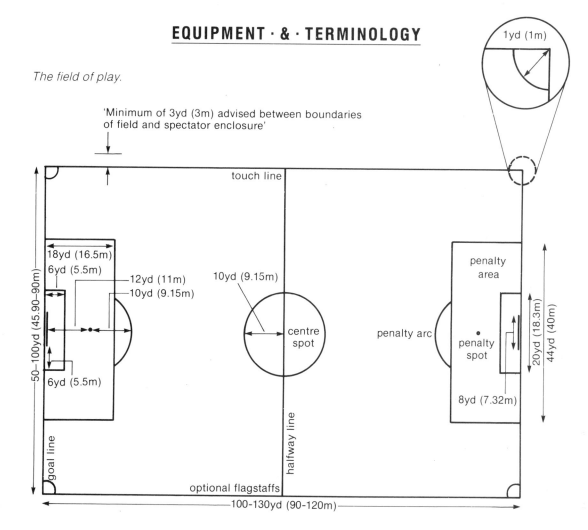

touch line

18yd (16.5m)
6yd (5.5m)
12yd (11m)
10yd (9.15m)
10yd (9.15m)
6yd (5.5m)

50–100yd (45.90–90m)

centre spot

penalty arc

penalty area

penalty spot

20yd (18.3m)
44yd (40m)

8yd (7.32m)

goal line

halfway line

optional flagstaffs

100-130yd (90-120m)

goalposts. They extend into the field of play for a distance of 6yd (5.5m) and are joined by a line parallel to the goal-line. This area defines the goal area. The goal area is enclosed within the larger penalty area. This is created by drawing two lines at right-angles to the goal-line 18yd (16.5m) from each goal post and extending into the field of play a distance of 18yd (16.5m). They are joined by a line parallel to the goal-line.

The penalty spot, from where penalty kicks are taken, is marked 12yd (11m) from the goal-line and facing the mid-point of the goal. As the Laws decree all players must stand 10yd (9.15m) from the ball when a penalty kick is taken, and must stand

outside the penalty area; an arc with a radius of 10yd (9.15m), using the penalty spot as its centre, is drawn outside the penalty area.

The ball

The ball is round and made of leather or any other approved material. Its circumference should be between 27–28in (0.68–0.71m) and weigh between 14–16oz (396–453gm).

The goals

Situated at each end of the field as already outlined, each goal consists of two uprights placed 8yd (7.32m) apart (the inside measurement between the two posts) and

The ball.

27-28in (69-71cm)

joined at the top by a crossbar 8ft (2.44m) (to the lower part of the bar) above the ground.

The uprights and crossbar should not exceed 5in (0.12m) in width and should all be the same width. Uprights are normally made of wood but can be made of tubular steel. Nets are normally fitted to the back of the uprights and crossbar, so as to clearly indicate when a goal has been scored. In matches without nets, disputes often arise as to whether a ball has crossed the goal-line inside or outside the goal. If you are the goalkeeper of a poor team, nets will save you a lot of time chasing balls after each goal.

Player's equipment

Players of the same team all wear the same colour shirt, except for the goalkeeper who should be distinctive, but must not wear a shirt the same colour as the opposing team or referee. Naturally, if two teams wear the same colour shirts one of them has to change. The rules of each competition dictate which. In the Football League it is the away team. Players of the same team must also wear identical shorts and socks, and be numbered according to their position on the field. The standard numbering system is:

1 – Goalkeeper	7 – Forward/midfielder
2 – Full back	8 – Striker/defender
3 – Full back	9 – Striker
4 – Midfielder/defender	10 – Striker/defender
5 – Central defender	11 – Forward/midfielder
6 – Midfielder/defender	12+ Substitutes

Players wear boots with either nylon, rubber or moulded studs which must not be dangerous to another player. For playing on an artificial surface, or in conditions where the ground is hard, rubber-soled shoes are preferable.

SOCCER · TERMINOLOGY

Advantage clause   The referee can, at his discretion, allow play to continue after a foul has been committed if he feels the offended team would be further punished by stopping play.

Blind side   The side of a player behind whom either an opponent runs or the ball is played whilst his attention is drawn in the opposite direction.

Booking   The act of the referee of taking a player's name following a serious breach of the Laws. If a player commits two 'bookable' offences in a game he is automatically sent off the field. Also called a caution.

Caution   See *Booking*.

Centre   (also known as a *cross*) . . . the act of a player kicking the ball towards the penalty area from the touchlines.

The goal.

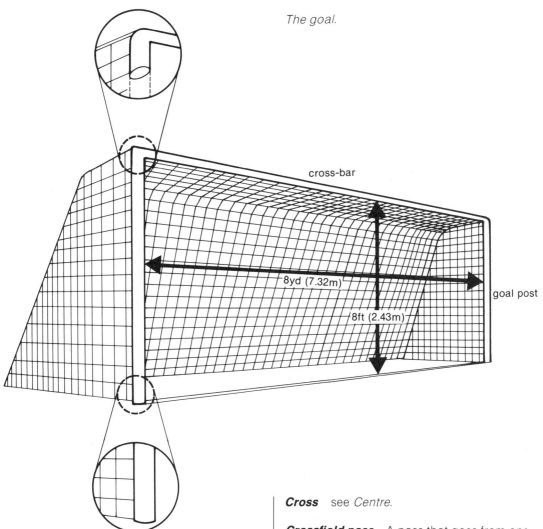

cross-bar

8yd (7.32m)

8ft (2.43m)

goal post

Cross   see *Centre.*

Crossfield pass   A pass that goes from one side of the pitch to the other in an effort to split and confuse the defence or set up an attack.

Chip   A kick made with backspin, especially useful for an attacking team from a free kick to embarrass the defensive 'wall'.

Dead Ball   When the ball is kicked from a stationary position, i.e. free kick, goal kick, etc.

Covering   When a player commits himself to a tackle, a fellow defender will cover his position on the field in case he is unsuccessful with the tackle.

Defender   One of the back players whose job it is to prevent opposing players from getting into scoring positions, and also to protect their own goalkeeper.

The goal area.

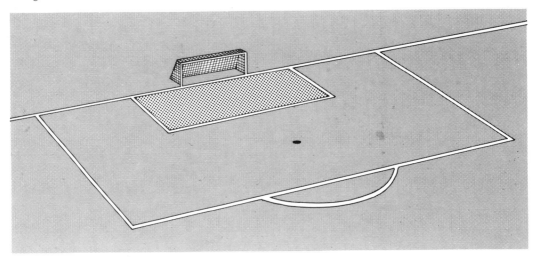

Defensive wall At a free kick near to the goal the defence will create a wall of players to prevent the opposing team gaining an advantage. The wall must line up a minimum 10yd (9.15m) from where the kick is taken.

Extra time If the scores are level at the end of ninety minutes and it is necessary to find a winner a period of extra time is played. It normally constitutes two halves each lasting fifteen minutes.

Far post The goal post furthest away from the attacker in possession of the ball.

Free kick Following an infringement, play is re-started with a free kick by the non-offending team. The kick will either be direct or indirect depending upon the nature of the offence. A goal can be scored from a direct free kick without another player touching the ball, but not from an indirect free kick.

Goal difference The difference between the number of goals a team scores and concedes during a season.

Kick-off The action of starting the game, or re-starting it at the commencement of the second half, or after each goal, is a kick-off.

Killing the ball When a player makes the ball stationary, either by trapping or other means, he has 'killed' the ball.

Marking Marking is done by keeping close to an opposing player thus making it difficult for him to get away from you, or for one of his team-mates to make a pass to him.

Midfielder A player who operates in the middle of the field. He is the link man between the defence and the attack.

Near post The goal post nearest to the position of the ball.

Offside When an attacking player receives the ball from a forward pass and there are less than two defenders between him and

The Dutch international Johann Cruyff, in the twilight of his sparkling career at New York Cosmos.

the goal line at the time. The offside rule is fully explained in the rules chapter on page 23.

Overlapping   When a player, normally a full back, goes past a team-mate along the touchline to take up an attacking position.

Over the top   A tackle 'over the top' of the ball is a dangerous one, and one that referees keep a careful eye open for.

Penalty kick   A direct free kick at the goal from the penalty spot as the result of an infringement in the penalty area.

Penalty shoot-out   A method of determining the winning team if teams are level at the end of ninety minutes and a period of extra-time. Players take alternate penalties at the opposing goalkeepers and try to score. The team with the most extra goals after five attempts each are the winners. If still level it becomes a sudden-death shoot-out thereafter. Goals scored in a penalty shoot-out are not credited to the team's score from the normal ninety minutes plus extra time played.

Running off the ball   The art of an attacking player without possession of the ball moving into space to receive a pass from one of his team-mates.

Selling a dummy   Faking the direction of a dribble or pass to confuse a defender.

Set piece   A pre-determined and much rehearsed move by the attacking team from dead-ball situations – free kicks, corner kicks, etc.

Square pass   A pass made laterally across the pitch is a square pass.

Striker   The all-out attacking player whose job it is to score goals.

Sweeper   The defender who operates behind the last line of defenders.

Tactical foul   A foul deliberately committed in order to gain an advantage, often to prevent a probable scoring situation.

Through ball   A defence-splitting pass to an attacker running towards the goal.

THE GAME – A GUIDE

Association Football, commonly known as 'soccer', is a game played by two teams, each consisting of eleven players, one of whom must be a goalkeeper. He must wear clothing that distinguishes him from his team-mates and does not clash with the colours worn by his opponents. Substitutes are permitted, but once a man has been replaced, he may not re-enter the game. The rules of each competition dictate how many named substitutes per side are permitted but a large number of leagues allow two. In competitive international soccer it is the normal practice for a panel of five substitutes to be named before a match, any two of whom may be used during the game, but in many 'friendly' internationals more than two substitutes can be used, subject to prior agreement between the teams.

The game is governed by seventeen 'Laws' and regulated on the pitch by a referee, normally supported by two linesmen. These officials are also responsible for implementing the eighteenth and 'unwritten' law – common sense.

Basically, soccer is a very simple game, hence its immense popularity. The object is to propel a ball by foot, or indeed by any part of the body except the hands or arms, into your opponents' goal.

Scoring is measured in goals, and to score a goal the whole of the ball must pass between the goalposts, under the crossbar and across the line (which is in fact part of the playing area's perimeter line). The team scoring the most goals during the match is the winner. If no goals are scored or the teams score an equal number of goals, the match is termed a 'draw'. In certain competitions where a draw is unacceptable and a winner needs to be found, there may be provision for a period of extra time to be played, normally fifteen minutes each half. And if this produces no result there may be a replay on another day or a 'penalty shoot-out'.

In such a shoot-out each team takes five penalty kicks at their opponents' goal with a different player taking each kick in turn. If this fails to separate the teams, they continue taking alternate penalty kicks until one team has the advantage.

To start the game, each team's captain (who is appointed from among the eleven players starting the game) meets the referee, normally in the centre circle, for the toss of a coin. Usually, the home team's captain spins the coin and the away team's captain calls. The winner then decides whether to elect to kick-off or to choose ends for the first half (the teams change ends at the half-time interval).

The referee is normally dressed all in black, although other colour schemes are

The penalty area.

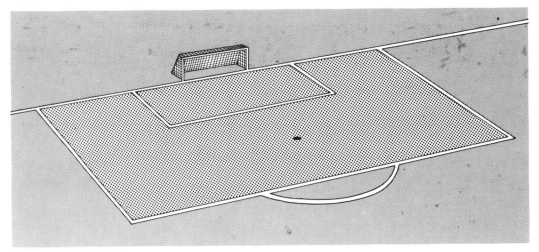

sometimes used. The important thing is that his clothing must not bear any resemblance to that worn by either team. He will take onto the pitch with him a whistle, a notepad and a watch. In professional football it is essential that a good stopwatch is used, and top class referees will carry two watches with them . . . batteries do have a habit of running out!

In most professional games these days the referee also carries two coloured cards – a yellow one which he holds aloft to indicate that a player has been officially cautioned or 'booked', and a red one which indicates that a player is being dismissed from the game. These cards are used in the event of certain infringements of the Laws, which are discussed later in this chapter.

At the start of the game, the teams are positioned in their respective halves and take up position in any one of a number of possible formations. A typical opening gambit would see the ten outfield players arranged in three lines – either four defenders, four midfielders and two attackers (4-4-2, a common line-up for the away team) or four defenders, three midfielders and three attackers (4-3-3, a common starting line-up for the home team).

The goalkeeper is normally confined to the penalty area, where he is able to handle the ball. He is allowed to come out of the area, at his peril, but he must not use his hands or arms when he does so. Normally he will only leave his area in an emergency – for example to race out and kick a ball away before an opposing attacker has the chance to take possession of it.

The game starts with the kick-off. The ball is placed on the centre spot and kicked by one of the attackers. The ball is deemed to be in play once it has travelled a distance equivalent to its own circumference, and the player taking the kick-off may not play the ball again until it has been touched by another player. The ball must travel forward initially (i.e. into the opponents' half of the field) and none of the opposing players may be within 10yd (9.15m) of the ball at the moment it is kicked off. In other words, they must not only be in their own half of the field (as must the players of the team taking the kick-off) but also outside the ten-yard radius of the centre circle. This procedure is repeated at the start of the second half. Teams change ends at half-time and the team who did NOT kick off in the first half do so in the second. Play also re-starts with a kick-off after each goal has been scored. The team conceding the goal kicks off.

The duration of the game is normally ninety minutes, although this may be reduced slightly in school or other junior football, and play is divided into two equal halves each lasting forty-five minutes. At half time there is an interval which is a minimum of five minutes, although this may be extended by permission of the referee and usually amounts to between ten and fifteen minutes in professional soccer.

In addition to the ninety minutes playing time the referee, who is the only official timekeeper involved in the game, has absolute discretion to add time at the end of each half to compensate for time lost through time-wasting tactics or through an injury to a player or players. If a penalty kick should be awarded at the end of a half, time is allowed for the taking of the kick.

As football is a sport involving a good deal of physical contact, infringement of the Laws will inevitably occur during play, and the referee has the responsibility of enforcing these Laws.

He may penalize the offending team by awarding a free kick or, in certain circumstances, a penalty kick. However, he may decide to allow play to continue if he considers that to do otherwise would result in a further disadvantage to the offended team. This is usually referred to as 'playing the advantage'. Even if he plays the advantage, the referee may subsequently caution the offending player when the ball next goes out of play.

The kick-off.

SOCCER

Indirect and direct free kicks.

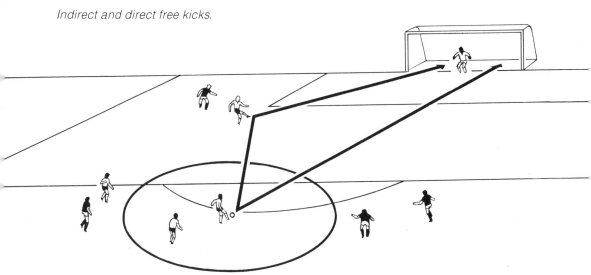

Free kicks may be either 'direct' or 'indirect'. The difference is that a goal may be scored directly from a direct free kick, but not from an indirect free kick, where a player other than the one who took the kick (either from his own team or the opposing team) must play the ball before a goal can be scored. Generally speaking, direct free kicks are awarded for the more serious offences, and indirect free kicks for the less serious ones. All free kicks (except penalties) are taken from the place where the infringement occurred, and the defending team's players must be at least 10yd (9.15m) from the ball at the moment it is kicked, although the side taking the kick has the option of waiving this rule should they consider that they would obtain greater advantage from taking the kick quickly. In all cases, the person taking the kick must not touch the ball again until it has been played by another player, and the ball must travel the length of its own circumference before it is deemed to be in play.

The more serious offences, for which a direct free kick can be awarded, are for *intentional* fouls or misconduct, and are divided into nine categories, eight of which are fouls against another player, and one technical. The eight are:

1 kicking or attempting to kick an opponent;
2 tripping or throwing an opponent;
3 jumping at an opponent;
4 charging an opponent from behind (unless he is obstructing you);
5 striking or attempting to strike or spit at an opponent;
6 holding an opponent;
7 pushing an opponent;
8 charging an opponent in a violent or dangerous manner.

The ninth offence is that of handling the ball deliberately, which is defined as carrying, propelling or striking the ball with the hand or arm. The goalkeeper is, of course, exempt from the rule . . . providing he is inside the penalty area at the time he handles the ball. If an outfield player *accidentally* handles the ball or is struck on the hand or arm by the ball in circumstances where the referee believes he could not have avoided contact, this does not constitute a foul.

If any of these nine offences is committed by the defending side in its own penalty area, the referee will award a penalty, which is taken from the penalty spot. For the taking of a penalty the goalkeeper must stand on his own goal-line, and must not move his feet until the ball is struck.

The penalty can be awarded irrespective of where the ball is at the time the offence is committed, provided the ball is in play and the offence takes place in the penalty area. Indeed, committing a foul on an opponent after the ball has gone is considered particularly serious. Naturally a goal may be scored direct from a penalty. The only players allowed in the penalty area until the ball has been kicked are the one taking the kick and the goalkeeper. If either team infringe these regulations, the kick will be re-taken, except in the case of an infringement by the defending team in cases where the ball has entered the goal. In this case a goal will normally be awarded, because to do otherwise would be to allow the offending team to gain advantage from the infringement. After all, if the kick is re-taken, the player taking the kick may miss on the second occasion.

There are a further set of offences which are punished by the award of an indirect free kick. The six main ones are:

1 dangerous (rather than violent) play;
2 charging fairly but at a time when the opponent does not have the ball within playing distance;
3 obstruction;
4 charging the goalkeeper except when he is holding the ball or is obstructing an opponent, or has passed outside his goal-area;
5 time-wasting by the goalkeeper;
6 penalizing the goalkeeper for taking more than four steps whilst in possession of the ball, including releasing it inside his own penalty area to a colleague and then re-possessing it before it has passed outside the penalty area.

The referee should distinguish the award of an indirect free kick by raising one arm above his head and keeping it there until the ball has been touched by a second player.

Indirect free kicks are also awarded for breaches of what is the most controversial and hotly-debated Law of all – offside.

The penalty kick.

SOCCER

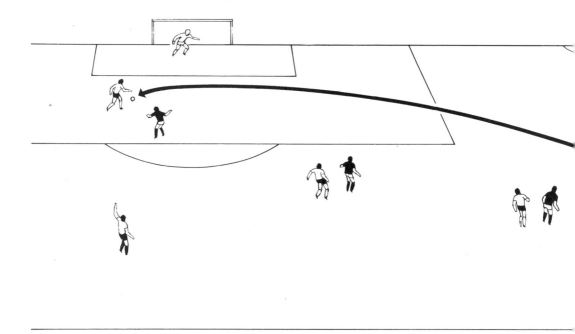

Offside is unique within the Laws of soccer, because it is the only way in which a defending side may attempt to prevent their opponents from scoring without touching the ball or using their bodies. Perhaps this is the reason why this Law seems to be so widely misunderstood. The Law has been varied and modified over the years, but whether you take the positive view of it and regard it as a Law designed to prevent the game becoming a sort of 'ping-pong', with lobs into a packed goalmouth from either end of the field, or a negative view which might regard it as a Law which compresses play into the central area of the field of play, it is undoubtedly the hardest rule for the players and the spectators to comprehend and for the referee to interpret.

Basically, the Law states: 'a player is offside if he is nearer his opponents' goal-line than the ball at the moment the ball is last played, unless . . .' and then follow four basic exceptions:

(a) the player is in his own half of the field;

(b) two or more of his opponents are between him and their goal-line (usually one of these is the goalkeeper, though this is not necessary);

(c) the ball last touched an opponent or was last played by him;

(d) the ball is received direct from a goal kick, a corner kick, a throw-in or when dropped by the referee.

In respect of exception (c), it is important to note that if a player is in an offside position, and interfering with play or an opponent, he cannot be played onside if the ball merely touches an opponent during its flight.

The referee's discretion is crucial to the enforcement of this Law, because if he deems that an attacking player, albeit in an offside position, is not interfering with play or with an opponent, or seeking to gain an advantage by being in an offside position, then he need not penalize.

Offside! Player 1 has only one defender – the goalkeeper – between him and the goal-line at the moment the ball is played.

kick. It is normally the goalkeeper's job to take goal kicks, but not compulsory.

The **corner kick** is used when any member of the defending team plays the ball over the goal-line (except through the goal itself). A quarter-circle with a radius of 1yd (1m) is drawn in each of the four corners of the field, and the ball must be placed within that quadrant at the end of the defending side's goal-line nearest to where the ball went out of play. A member of the attacking team then kicks the ball into play. As with kick-offs and free kicks, the person taking the kick may not touch the ball a second time until it has touched another player. Defenders must not encroach within 10yd (9.15m) of the quadrant until the ball has been kicked.

The **throw in** is used to re-start play when the ball crosses either touch line. A member of the team opposing that whose player last touched the ball before it crossed the touch-line takes the ball in both hands and throws it back into play from behind and over his head. This is the only occasion when a player other than the goalkeeper may use his hands during the game. The player taking the throw must do so as close as possible to the point at which the ball crossed the line (such judgement is usually made by the referee or linesman), he must face the pitch and he must have both feet on the ground, on or behind the touch-line at the moment he delivers the throw.

The importance of the corner flag posts can be seen here inasmuch as they help the referee or linesmen to determine whether a throw-in or corner kick/goal kick should be awarded on the occasion when the ball crosses the boundary line in the immediate vicinity of the corner of the field of play.

The field of play, as already described, incorporates boundary lines. When the ball passes over these boundary lines, play has to stop and be re-started in some way. Re-starting can be by one of five methods:

   1 with a kick-off;
   2 with a goal kick;
   3 with a corner kick;
   4 with a throw-in;
   5 with a dropped-ball.

The **goal kick** is used when the ball crosses the goal-line (except when it goes in the goal itself) and was last played by a member of the attacking team. The defending side then re-start the game by kicking the ball out from that half of their goal area nearest to where the ball crossed the goal-line. The ball is not deemed to be in play until it has passed out of the penalty area, and if a player of either team plays the ball before it has passed out of the penalty area, the kick must be retaken. A goal may not be scored direct from a goal

The **dropped-ball** is the only method of restarting the game which does not have the whole of an individual Law assigned to it. Where the referee is forced to stop play for

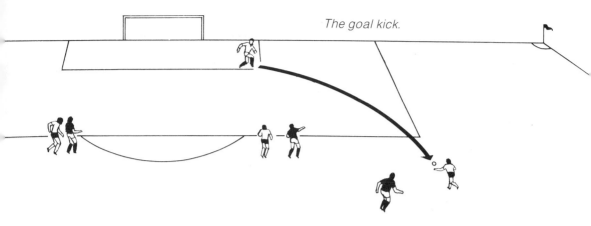

The goal kick.

reasons other than the deliberate act of a player (for example, where a player has been accidentally injured and the injury appears to be so serious that the referee decides to stop the game so that the player can receive immediate attention) he will re-start the play by dropping the ball at a point where it was when he suspended play. The ball is deemed to be in play at the moment it touches the ground, and no player may play or attempt to play the ball until that moment. One player from each team stands on either side of the referee when he drops the ball, and if either of them does touch the ball before it hits the ground, the drop will be re-taken.

Finally, Laws have been framed to deal with serious foul play, persistant offenders and ungentlemanly conduct towards the opposition, the match officials and even members of the same team. There are a number of such situations where a player should be cautioned by the referee, and in this context 'cautioning' means entering the offending player's name in the referee's notebook (hence the common use of the term 'booking a player') and subsequently reporting him to the authority under whose jurisdiction the match is played.

The situations where a player would be cautioned under these Laws are:

1 entering or leaving the field of play without receiving a signal from the referee to do so;
2 persistently infringing the Laws of the game;

The corner kick.

3 showing, by words or actions, dissent from any decision given by the referee;
4 ungentlemanly conduct.

This last offence (4) which is assessed by the referee, covers a multitude of footballing sins.

For even more serious offences, a player shall be sent off the field if, in the opinion of the referee, he is guilty of violent conduct or serious foul play, including spitting at an opponent, the use of foul or abusive language, or persistent misconduct after having been cautioned. In the case of cautionable offences where the game is stopped for the referee to administer the caution, it is restarted by an indirect free kick. The same applies to a sending-off offence, although in both cases the game would be started by a direct free kick if the stoppage was caused by an offence which normally results in a direct free kick.

The throw-in.

RULES CLINIC

At set pieces, the opposition have to be ten yards from the ball. Does this apply at a dropped-ball?

No. The ball is usually dropped between two players – one from each team. However, this does not have to be so, since the Law merely states that the ball has to touch the ground when dropped by the referee at the place where play had been suspended. Theoretically, he could drop it with several players around, or with none, but the ball must not be played by any player until it touches the ground. In practice the ball is dropped as indicated between only two players (one from each team) to avoid a free-for-all scrimmage and the likely infringement of the Laws which would result.

Can a goalkeeper score a goal?

Most certainly yes. He can score with a kick from his hands from his own penalty area, provided the ball is in play, or he can come out of his penalty area (at which point he is treated as an ordinary outfield player) then dribble up the field and shoot, or he can score from set pieces such as penalties (which does happen from time to time) or corners (unlikely, but possible). What he cannot do is score from a goal kick from his own goal area, as this is one restart from which no-one can score.

What constitutes the offence of obstruction?

This is normally described as the interposition of the body between the ball and an opponent when the ball is not within playing distance and there is no attempt to play the ball.

When the defending side has a free kick inside its own penalty area, is it sufficient for the ball to travel merely the distance of its own circumference before being deemed 'in play'?

No. This is an exception to the rule since in this instance the ball must travel outside the penalty area in order to be in play. If it does not, the kick must be retaken. A similar provision applies at goal kicks.

If the ball is played to an attacker in his own half of the field, but there are fewer than two defenders between him and his opponents' goal-line, is he offside?

No. A player cannot be offside in his own half of the field. The same point applies if the ball is played into the defending side's half of the field and the attacker runs from his own half of the field into his opponents' half of the field *after* the ball has been played.

Are the lines marking out the field of play inside or outside the areas they bound?

The space within the inside areas of the field of play includes the width of the lines marking these areas. The width of the lines must not exceed 5in (0.12m). The lines therefore belong to the areas of which they are the boundaries, and so touch-lines and goal-lines, for example, are part of the field of play.

What is the decision if only a part of the ball crosses the boundary line?

The decision would be to continue play, because the ball is only out of play when the whole of the ball has crossed the line, either on the ground or in the air.

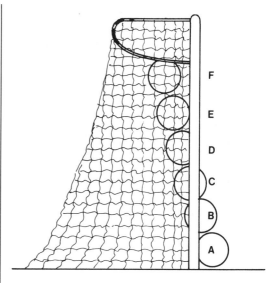

Only balls E and F count as goals.

In play.   Out of play.

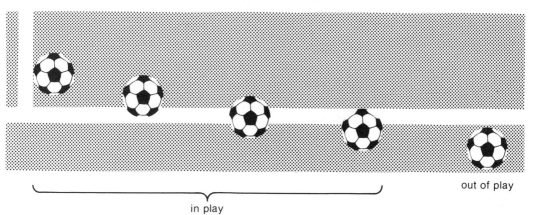

in play

out of play

Can you be offside if you are behind the ball and it is passed back to you?

No. A player must be nearer to his opponents' goal-line than the ball at the moment the ball is last played, so if the ball is played backwards rather than forwards, it stands to reason that the receiver cannot be offside.

If an attacker shoots when one of his team-mates is standing in an offside position and the ball hits a defender and is deflected to the player who is offside, is he played onside by the fact that the ball was last played or touched by a defender?

For many years, he would have been played onside in such a situation, but the Laws

have now been amended so that such a player can never be played onside. Of course, if he receives the ball via a misdirected pass from a defender, he will be onside, but such a pass is a voluntary act, and a deflection is not. Where, for example, a player is standing in an offside position well out of the line of vision of the defenders – particularly the defending goalkeeper – and the attacker shoots, or passes to an onside colleague in another direction, the referee will normally use his discretion to allow play to continue, because the offside attacker is neither interfering with play or an opponent, nor seeking to gain an advantage by being in that position.

If a player is onside when the ball is played, but has moved into an offside position by the time he receives the ball, is he offside?

No. A player is not offside when he receives the ball, but the decision is judged from the moment that the ball is passed to him by any member of his own team.

What constitutes hand-ball?

This is a deliberate act whereby the player strikes the ball with any part of his hand or arm. Unfortunately, the Law does not state precisely where the arm ends, so it is usually assumed to go as far as the shoulder. Where the ball accidentally strikes the hand or arm, no offence is committed. The goalkeeper can, of course, handle the ball in his own penalty area as a matter of right under the Laws, but clearly not in his opponents' penalty area!

Maradona of Argentina (with the beard), outwits the French midfield player Jean Tigana, during a 'friendly' international match played in Paris in March 1986.

Can you score an own goal from a free kick awarded to your team?

No. A goal can only be scored by the attacking side against the defending side at a direct free kick. If the ball goes into the goal, the referee would award a corner against the defending side, and not an own goal.

If the ball goes into the goal from an indirect free kick without touching another player, what happens?

It is NOT a goal, and play re-starts with a goal kick.

If a player is injured, is he allowed to receive treatment on the field?

This depends on the seriousness of the injury. The Laws provide for the referee to stop the game in case of serious injury, have the player removed from the field of play and resume the game as quickly as possible. If a player is slightly injured, the game should not be stopped, but in practice it normally is, especially in the case of head injuries. Treatment is also normally allowed on the pitch in cases of minor injuries, but referees will be alert to ensure that no liberties are taken. Note that a goalkeeper may be changed not only for injury but for tactical reasons, but the referee must be notified before this takes place. A player returning after injury must receive a signal from the referee, and this can be done even while the game is in play, but a substitution may only be made when the ball is 'dead'.

Can the ball be changed during play?

Yes – with the authorization of the referee. This is unlikely to occur unless the ball goes out of shape or bursts, as it did in the first two FA Cup finals after the Second World War, or becomes dangerous to the players because of deflation or weight increase.

Sometimes the referee will see fit to change the ball to one of a different colour during the game because of a change in weather conditions – most usually a sudden snowfall. Where the ball is 'mislaid' (e.g. kicked over the stand roof or appropriated by a spectator) a replacement may be used, but if the original ball is then returned, it must be used, provided it is in a fit condition.

What happens at a penalty kick if either the goalkeeper moves before the kick is taken or a defender encroaches into the penalty area?

The referee will await the result of the kick, and if the attacker scores, he will award a goal. If the kick fails, he will order it to be retaken. It should also be noted that the attacker must not stop and restart during his run-up or behave in any manner calculated to make the goalkeeper move too soon (such as feinting the kick). If the attacking side encroaches and the kick is successful, the referee will order it to be retaken. If members of *both* the attacking and defending sides encroach at the same time, the kick will be retaken regardless of whether it is successful or not.

If a player takes a penalty kick and the ball rebounds to him from the crossbar or the goalposts, can he score at the second attempt?

No. The goal will not stand, and an indirect free kick will be awarded against the penalty kicker's team for the offence of playing the ball twice at a 'dead-ball' kick. Note that had the ball rebounded after striking the referee, the same result would ensue, since the referee is regarded as 'football furniture' for this purpose. If the ball had gone in directly off the posts, the bar or indeed the referee, the goal would therefore stand. The kicker can strike the ball if it rebounds to him after touching the goalkeeper, since it has been 'played' by a second player and is deemed to be in play.

What is the function of the referee in soccer?

His is one of the most important functions, since he is there to enforce the Laws, keep a record of the game, act as timekeeper, and interpret the actions of the players in terms of whether they are acting within the Laws and pass judgement and sentence on them when they are not. He will use his discretion to allow the advantage when the ball remains in play, but once he has signalled such intention to keep the game moving, he may not subsequently change his mind. He may, however, caution a player the next time play stops, even though he has not punished the offence with a free kick.

However, the referee may change his decision in a dead-ball situation. For example, if he awards a goal and his attention is subsequently drawn to something he had not been aware of (e.g. by a linesman pointing out an offence which had not been seen by the referee), he can then disallow the goal, provided that the game has not been restarted.

The referee must wear colours which distinguish him from the players, use his whistle in an intelligent manner and utilize the official signals laid down by the governing body, FIFA. He has full authority from the first whistle to the last, and sometimes even longer, and a good referee will try to encourage the spirit of the game as well as enforcing the laws, which will mean that he will try to keep the game flowing and to ensure that the players and spectators enjoy the game.

What are the functions of the linesmen?

The majority of football played throughout the world is termed 'junior football' and is played either with no linesmen or with so-called 'club linesmen', who are usually provided by the participating teams. However, where official linesmen are appointed, they will be neutral, two in number and qualified referees in their own right. Their function is to assist the referee in the execution of his duties, and they have responsibility for determining when the ball goes out of play for a throw-in, goal kick or corner kick. They will also, by signalling with their flags, advise the referee as to which team should get the decision. They are especially important when it comes to determining offside decisions, and will also bring to the referee's attention an infringement of the Laws which has taken place outside the referee's field of vision.

How do the referee and linesmen perform their function of control?

The referee patrols the pitch in one of several different ways, while the linesmen patrol the touch-lines. Referees normally run what is called a 'diagonal' system, whereby he sticks approximately to one of the imaginary diagonal lines between the corners. The linesmen, meanwhile, run half a touch-line each, diagonally opposite to each other, and the referee will decide which diagonal they adopt. He will then run the other diagonal, and will always keep one linesman in sight.

Recently, some referees have taken to running a Z pattern in order to give themselves greater width and vision. The Russians have pioneered a system called the 'linear' system, whereby the referee patrols the whole length of one side of the pitch and the linesmen run the touch-line on the other side, taking half each. This system has never really found widespread acceptance, except by referees who have no linesmen, where it can be better than running a diagonal. Experiments have been carried out with a two-referee system with no linesmen, each referee being responsible for one half of the field and assisting his colleague in the other, but this system has no official status. The diagonal system is generally accepted to be perfectly effective and has served the game well for many years.

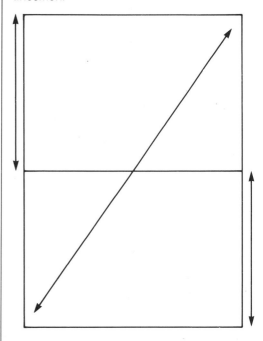

Diagonal coverage by the referee and linesmen.

In women's football, can a lady be guilty of ungentlemanly conduct?

Most certainly. The Laws have been codified in such a way that only the masculine gender is referred to, and no official mention is made within the Laws about women's football, but the game is now governed world-wide by one body, and there is one set of Laws which clearly apply to both sexes. Strangely, mixed football is not officially permitted!

TECHNIQUE

If football, as it is often claimed, is such a simple game with simple objectives, how is it that the game becomes complicated or difficult? The answer is itself very simple. It is because the attacking player faces three problems. The first is his own lack of either technique or skill; the second are the natural elements which go to make up the game such as the pitch, the weather or the climatic effect on the ball; and the third and probably most important is the standard of the opposing team, who will have the same objectives in mind and seek to achieve them either by a higher level of technique or skill or by the use of legitimate tactical ploys, particularly in relation to team formations or dead-ball restarts.

There are, arguably, only eight major elements to playing soccer, six of which relate to outfield players in general, one to the specialist position of goalkeeper, and one to team organization. These eight elements are as follows:

1 Passing
2 Ball control
3 Shooting
4 Running, both with and without the ball
5 Winning the ball
6 Heading
7 The speciality of goalkeeping
8 The team elements of set plays from restarts, both in attacking and defending situations.

Each of these elements in turn incorporate many facets in relation to technique and skills, which we will try to develop as far as is possible with words alone.

The words 'technique' and 'skill' have been defined in numerous ways, which include (for technique) 'the execution of a single performance' or 'the method of performance' and (for skill) 'the ability and judgement to select the correct technique on demand' or 'the performance of a function when under pressure from opponents'. For the purposes of this book, technique is defined here as the correct performance of a footballing function, whilst skill will be defined merely as the honing or perfecting of a footballing function either with or without the presence of an opponent.

Although statistics were compared with 'lies and damned lies' by Sir Winston Churchill, reliance must be placed upon them from time to time, provided of course that sensible conclusions are drawn from them. Accordingly, since many studies and tests have been run by numerous people and bodies, including the English Football Association, due regard must be given to some of these findings, especially those which have recorded the average time each player spends in possession of the ball during a match. One study showed that in the English First and Second Divisions over a period of some four years, the ball was actually in play for only between fifty-four and sixty-four minutes out of ninety. Statistics compiled during the World Cup final tournament in 1978 supported these findings, and also indicated that the skill of

The great George Best, at the height of his considerable powers with Manchester United.

the players was a vital factor in determining the amount of time the ball was in play. In short, the less skilful the players, the more the ball failed to stay within the playing area.

Taking rough averages from various studies, it would seem that unless a team is playing the ball repeatedly to one or two special players, each outfield player will have possession of the ball for no more than between two and four minutes during the course of a match. These figures for ball in play in general and players on the ball in particular will alter downwards the more junior the football becomes, especially so at 'park' or school football levels.

The obvious conclusion to be drawn from these statistics is that it is vitally important to develop as high a level of skill as possible, in order to maximize the playing time and therefore the opportunities to create and score goals.

Soccer is essentially a game of good habits, which hopefully are learned as early and as young as possible. It is helpful, in relation to the eight basic elements of the game mentioned at the start of this chapter, to remember some little catch-phrases, and so we will now deal with each of the eight elements in turn.

PASSING

If you can't pass, you can't play

This is a catch-phrase frequently used by coaches when trying to teach one of the most important of all soccer skills. Passing involves not only your foot, but also your chest and frequently your head, and even other parts of your body may be used.

However, your feet are certainly the most important parts of the anatomy in relation to passing, and so it is the use of one or both feet which will be stressed here. It is important to remember from the outset that there are three parts of your foot which are used in passing: the inside and widest part

of your foot, the instep or front of the foot and, most frequently overlooked, the outside of the foot. In British soccer the inside and instep are the parts most commonly used for passing, but many European and South American players have reached high levels of skill in the use of the outside of the foot to disguise the intended direction of the pass and also to swerve the ball through the air.

Accuracy in passing is clearly the paramount consideration, and, to return to statistics, studies carried out in England have shown that an astonishingly high number of passes go astray during professional matches. It is not surprising, therefore, that the lower down the football scale you go, the lower the percentage of accurate passes that you see. In one study of junior football it was found that seven out of every ten passes went astray, which actually meant that the best chance of receiving the ball in a dangerous position was to pass to the opposition, who would more frequently than not pass it straight back!

This situation cannot, of course, be tolerated when all the right conditions for match play exist. Passing is the building block of team play, so if a group of players want to achieve success as a team, they must pass accurately to each other.

A pass involves two players – one making the pass and the other receiving it – and three basic elements: weighting (the degree of power put into the pass), direction and timing. Properly combining these elements means that you should aim to send the ball to the position you anticipate your colleague being in at the moment he receives the ball. Particularly clever and accurate players can disguise their passes (thus reducing the chances of it being intercepted by the opposition) by showing an intention to play the ball one way and then playing it another, as in the 'reverse' pass.

As with all kicking (and this will be further discussed in the section dealing with shooting) there are a number of factors

The push pass

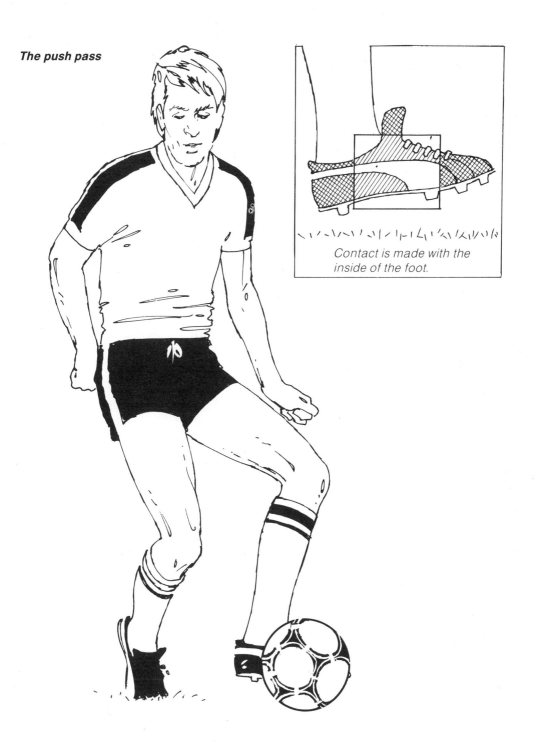

Contact is made with the
inside of the foot.

which remain constant. In order to pass or kick the ball on a low-level trajectory, the ball must be struck in a certain way. Low passing or kicking requires that the ball should be struck through its top half. To raise the ball above the ground, the ball has to be struck through its approximate middle line, and to loft the pass or indulge in the chip pass, the ball must be struck through its bottom half. As with many sports, the kicker's body position at the moment of strike is important in determining the direction and weight of the pass. In striking through the top of the ball you, as the kicker, will need to be close to the ball and put more weight into the kick, whereas to loft the ball you will need to be slightly farther back and get your foot under the ball to create the lever to gain the lift.

Although some players seem to be blessed with 'vision' or the insight necessary to be aware of the positioning of their colleagues and the opposition, which rare gift enables them to make particularly telling passes (you can't afford to spend much time looking around when you're in possession) even the greatest of players have to practise their passing constantly, and the first decision to be made is the selection of which part of the foot to use.

The commonest, and the one with which it is easiest to be accurate, is the pass with the inside of the foot, usually known as the 'push pass'. Depending on the power of the player and the needs of the occasion, this can be anything between five and thirty yards in length. Simple, quick and well-rehearsed passing always reaps dividends, especially if both the passer and the receiver have comfortable body positions and space at the time of making and receiving the pass. The right way needs little further explanation, but the wrong way has come to be known by the vivid term 'the hospital pass'. This is where a poor pass puts the receiver under such pressure from the opposition that he is in real danger of getting injured in his attempts to collect.

So the weighting of the pass is vital. Too weak, and it will not reach its target; too strong and it will either miss the target or be travelling too quickly for the receiver to control it.

The relative positions of the two players involved in the pass will normally determine what type of pass will be made. If general team-work is good and the passer has various team-mates to choose from, then options are increased, although the team's coach or manager may express a preference for certain passes in certain situations.

The field of play can be divided into roughly three equal portions for the purpose of narrowing down which type of pass is appropriate in certain situations. There is the defensive third, nearest to your own goal, the middle third and the attacking third. It is dangerous to take risks in your own defensive third, so defenders will frequently strike long balls out of defence. To do this, they will strike the ball with the instep, normally through the middle or bottom part of the ball. This is sometimes referred to as 'hitting the ball off the laces'. The

The field of play in thirds.

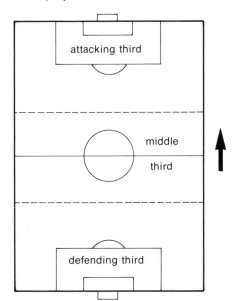

Hitting the ball off the laces.

non-kicking foot is placed next to the ball and the body tends to lean back, and the further the body leans back, the greater the height which will be achieved in the kick. There must be a good follow-through with your kicking foot and as with any pass, your head should be kept still and your eyes concentrated on the ball. This technique is also used to strike cross-field passes from one side of the field to the other and for centering the ball by crossing it from either flank when in the attacking third of the field. For the short pass, which can be used anywhere but is more frequently employed in the middle or attacking thirds of the field, the inside of your foot is most often used. Your toes are turned outwards so that the flat of the foot is exposed to the ball, and once again a good follow-through is necessary, striking through the middle or upper part of the ball. Your ankle joint is kept firm, your non-kicking foot is positioned alongside the ball, your head is kept down and usually your arms should be outstretched for good balance. However, any position in which you are comfortable and well-balanced will suffice, and it may not be necessary to have both arms outstretched.

Passing with the outside of your foot will assist in disguising a pass made on the run and has many other uses. The ball is struck centrally with your foot which is furthest forward and with your toes pointing inwards, but once again the ankle joint must be kept firm. Your non-kicking foot will be a little behind the kicking foot and further to the side than is the case with the pass made with the inside of your foot, and the usual follow-through along the line of the pass is essential.

With all good passing, the kicker has to keep his eye on the ball, but he must also be aware of the position of his team-mates before striking the pass. Therefore it is essential for the passer when about to receive the ball or when running with it to both look at the ball and keep his head up so that a rhythm is created in what is known as the 'split-glance'. This is particularly important when the passer intends to deliver the chipped pass. Here, the non-kicking foot is placed next to the ball, the body leans back and the ball is struck through its bottom half. Normally, the ball is struck off the laces, but clever players can chip a ball with both the inside and outside of their feet. In some cases, the ball can be cut from underneath with no follow-through, whilst to obtain a 'towering' chip there is a very neat follow-through. One variation is the 'knee-over' style, where the knee is bent forwards over the ball which is then chipped or stabbed from underneath.

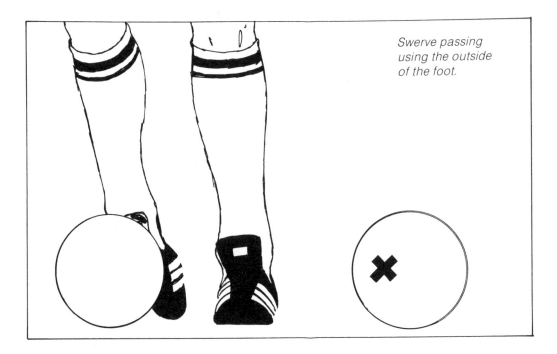

Swerve passing using the outside of the foot.

The more skilful players do not have to restrict themselves to passing the ball in a straight line. They will be able to bend the ball around opponents by striking it with either the inside or the outside of the foot. Spin is imparted to the ball by striking it off-centre and then following through at an angle to its intended path. Since in most cases the outer edge of the ball will be struck, the part of the foot which will perform the strike must be carefully selected, as must the line of approach to the ball.

Many of the passes already referred to relate to the passer having control of the ball, but there are times when he will be under pressure from an opponent or will be so astute that he will want to send the ball on to a colleague as soon as he receives it. This calls for what is known as the 'first time' pass. Here, the ball will be played at the moment it arrives, either with the foot, using any of the methods so far described, or even with the chest or head. The chest pass is achieved by thrusting your chest powerfully forward and letting the ball bounce off it to a colleague. The ball is passed downwards by getting your chest over the ball, and upwards by getting your chest underneath it. It stands to reason that it is difficult to impart a great deal of power to the ball in this way, so this method will normally be used only when the intended receiver is within close range, and such a pass will also be more effective if the ball is travelling at speed prior to being bounced off the chest.

The same principles apply to the headed pass, although somewhat greater power can be imparted to the ball in this way. In defence, the headed pass out to a colleague will usually follow an upward trajectory, directed away from goal, whereas in attack a flicked downward header or glancing header which changes the direction of the ball's flight to a relatively small degree will often create a scoring chance for a team-mate, or even result in a goal for the

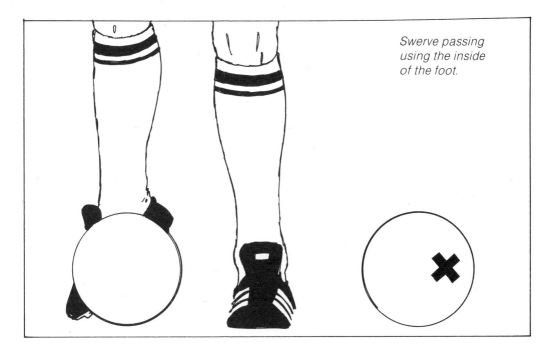

Swerve passing using the inside of the foot.

header. When heading the ball, the face is thrust forwards at the ball so that contact is made with the forehead, and it is important to get in line with the ball.

Both heading and volleying are dealt with in more detail later, but fine first-time passing can be achieved by the use of the volley or half-volley. Here, your non-kicking foot is alongside the ball, your body is brought into line, and you kick the ball in the required direction, adjusting your follow-through according to how much pace is required on the pass. Full volleys in particular require immaculate timing for maximum effectiveness.

Disguise can be achieved by pretending to pass in one direction and then actually passing in the opposite direction. This is often called the 'reverse pass'. Similar effect can be achieved by running over the ball and then flicking it back with your heel, and the 'back-heel' method of passing can also be used from a standing position.

There are numerous variations to passing, but to be successful, all the basic requirements must come into play, and the aim should always be to pass the ball forward at every opportunity, because that way lies your opponents' goal!

BALL-CONTROL –

Never lose your self-control

Perhaps the greatest aim of all players, especially from an individual point of view, is to gain mastery over the ball. To even begin to attempt this, you must be able to control it whenever and from wherever it comes to you, whether under pressure or in space. The most important factor in control is choosing the part of your body with which you intend to exercise the control and then getting that part in line with the ball.

The major 'control surfaces' are your foot,

*Preparing for a
wedge trap with
the outside of
the foot.*

TECHNIQUE

Cushion control with the instep.

thigh, chest and head, and the ball can either be stopped dead or, more often than not, directed at a pace and at an angle that you decide. Initial control of the ball always involves either 'trapping' or 'cushioning'. With trapping, you stop the ball dead, whilst with cushioning, the controlling surface (foot, thigh, chest or head) is relaxed slightly at the moment of impact, thus taking the pace or 'weight' off the ball.

Traditionally, trapping has been achieved by creating a wedge. The sole of your foot is lowered into position at an angle, heel down, your knee is bent and your whole body crouches forwards slightly. When the ball enters the trap or wedge thus created between the sole of your foot and the ground, it is stopped dead. There are a number of variations on this theme, using the inside or even the outside of your foot, but the principles remain the same. Only your angle of approach to the ball will vary according to which type of wedge trap is being attempted.

The wedge trap was highly favoured in Britain until the 1950s, when it slowly dawned on us that perhaps our footballing friends from overseas had rather better ideas. In that decade, more and more continental teams played over here and demonstrated the instep method of control. This is used when the ball is either crossed or comes at you from a height for any reason. Your instep is raised to meet the ball, and at the moment of impact your foot is withdrawn in the same direction as the ball is travelling, killing its pace with the cushioning effect described above. Very skilful players can actually catch the ball on their foot, and this trick can be varied to include control on either the inside or the outside of the foot.

This latter method is preferred to the wedge nowadays, because it is easier to move the ball off more quickly. The only way of moving the ball off quickly with the wedge is to actually raise and extend your leg so that the oncoming ball hits the sole of your foot and moves away in the required direction. As can be imagined, it is difficult to be accurate with this method.

The controls so far described depend to a great extent on the accuracy of the initial pass. If there's no time to move completely in line with the oncoming ball, it will be necessary to extend your leg upwards and outwards, controlling the ball with the inside of your foot. Very one-footed players may use their favoured leg to control the ball with

Prolific scorer Ian Rush exults in yet another great goal.

the outside of the 'wrong' foot in this situation, but this is an awkward business and it is better to learn to perform the simpler function with either foot.

Moving up the body, the next important control surface is your thigh. Here the same principles of getting in line with the ball, keeping your eye on it during its flight and cushioning are paramount. Your thigh must be angled to meet the oncoming ball, and there are several variations to this trap. Your arms play an important part in balancing, but because everyone's body balance is different, it is important to ascertain which position will give you the most comfortable balance. And you must decide whether you are going to kill the ball or move it on.

To kill a high ball, it is necessary to get underneath it as it falls, cushion the impact on your thigh by withdrawing the raised leg slightly and then allowing the ball to drop. The ball can also be caught on your thigh and even bounced there before allowing it to drop or volleying off a pass or a shot at goal.

With the ball coming straight at you, rather than dropping from a height, do not raise your knee but rather keep your thigh straight and bend your knee so that your lower leg is parallel to the ground. Cushion the ball as before, but then either allow it to drop or push it away with a punching movement of your thigh.

Chest control involves the frontal area of the trunk between your midriff and your neck. A dropping ball can be controlled with your chest angled upwards, either cushioning the ball and allowing it to drop, or thrusting your chest forwards to volley the

ball off, or your chest can be pointed downwards in order to direct the ball to the feet.

To receive the ball on the top of your chest, your arms should be outstretched to push your chest out and so create the largest possible area as a receiving surface. This will also help to arch your back. Your legs are planted firmly on the ground, and a cushioning effect is used as described above. It is possible to use variations of this method while on the run or jumping to meet the ball, but these are much more skilful techniques requiring considerable practice.

The hardest of all controls is the head trap. There is usually little time to perform this, and the ball often arrives at an awkward height or angle, so this is very much a 'last resort' method requiring great skill. It is even more vital than usual to get in line with the approaching ball, and your head is moved slightly forward to meet the ball. At the moment of impact, your head is moved backwards slightly in the direction of the ball's flight, and this produces the required cushioning effect. Often this method has to be used while you are in mid-jump, and this is an even more difficult procedure. Sometimes, you will have no choice but to prod the ball upwards and then let it fall, but if you have your feet on the ground at the moment of impact, you may also bend your knees to achieve the cushioning effect.

SHOOTING –

If you don't shoot, you won't score

The scoring of goals is arguably the most important of all aspects of soccer, but there is no difference between a spectacular goal and a scrambled one when it comes to the result of the match. All players prefer to score good-looking goals, but a team's leading goalscorer will usually accumulate most of his successful strikes with what are known as 'bread and butter' goals.

The chest trap.

Therefore, although it is important to both learn and know the best way to shoot, it is equally important to know where goals are scored from, where to aim, and why.

There are a number of statistics which show that the area around the far post is the one where most successful strikes originate. This area has been named by the Football Association's Assistant Director of Coaching as the 'position of maximum opportunity' or POMO for short. Whilst these statistics are unquestionably accurate, it must not be forgotten that the near post area will reap a rich reward – more so than might be imagined. The POMO will be effective because it tends to eliminate the goalkeeper and pull defenders out of position, but the near post will be effective because of the delay in the goalkeeper's movement to the danger and because defenders will normally be chasing back towards their own goal.

When shooting at goal, the old maxim of 'keep them low and in they go' should be remembered at all times. Shots which go high and over the bar are lost, whereas those aimed low, even if wide of the posts, may be diverted in by a colleague or even an opponent.

Much argument has raged over the years about where to direct shots to ensure success. The great Hungarian striker Puskas advocated aiming at the goalkeeper, because any inaccuracy will take the ball to one side of him. That is probably good advice for shots made under little pressure and from a central position, but under pressure, and with the ball moving across the goal or bouncing, it is probably better to aim just inside the far post. The advantage here is that if the goalkeeper or a defender touches the ball away, it may create a secondary strike opportunity for a colleague running in, or even allow the original striker to score from a rebound. Certainly all strikers should remember the wisdom of following up all potential rebounds – whether from your own shot or that of a colleague.

The most important aspect of all shooting and goalscoring efforts is the will or desire to shoot, and it is no coincidence, uncharitable though it may sound, that all top goalscorers are selfish. It is a fact of football life that unless you are prepared to shoot at every opportunity or even half-chance, you will not score many goals. It's simply a matter of deciding between the impossible, at which point you should clearly pass to a colleague who is in a better position to strike, and the possible, when it is always better to have a go yourself.

Having examined the principles of when and where to shoot, we should now look at 'how'.

It is wrong to lump all types of shots together. As with most techniques and skills in soccer, there are numerous variations. The ball will not always come to you as the striker along the ground at a perfect pace and angle. Indeed, this will happen only rarely. You will have to chase after the ball, either opposed or unopposed, intercept crosses arriving at different heights and angles, control balls which are bouncing high or low, or take 'knock-downs' from other players. Each time you must select quickly the shooting technique which is most appropriate. The higher the level of soccer, the less time you will have to do this. Then you must adjust your body accordingly, having glanced up quickly to sight the goal but otherwise keeping your eyes on the ball right on to your boot.

Knowing that the most effective shot is usually the low shot, you must apply the same basic principles as for a passing movement, although normally you will not have to judge the weight but simply drive the ball at full power. In other words, you must get the right angle of approach, a balanced, comfortable position, and, on contact with the ball, hit squarely through it along its middle or upper line. Usually, your instep should be used for this purpose, so that your toe is pointed down, your body leaning forward and your non-kicking foot placed alongside the ball. After contact there should

Shooting

Top left: The right angle of approach. Top right: Non-kicking foot alongside the ball, head down. Above: Good follow-through.

Volleying off the laces

Prepared and in line.

Good balance, head down.

be a good follow-through along the line of the shot to ensure maximum power.

As with the pass, there are variations available using the inside or outside of your foot to bend or swerve the ball, but these need a great deal of practice, and although they are certainly a very effective ploy and beautiful to watch when they work, such shots undoubtedly attract a higher percentage of misses than the more conventional method. Simplicity and certainty are better friends than speculation and the spectacular, but if you are good enough to achieve outstanding results with cunning shots, then by all means take advantage of the ability.

Since the ball will often come awkwardly to you, you must be able to drive the ball on the half-volley or full volley. For the half-volley, your shooting foot must be in line with the ball as it approaches, your body positioned over the ball at the moment of impact, and contact made as soon as possible after the ball has touched the

ground. Contact is made with that part of your foot selected for the strike, preferably on the mid-line of the ball. The line of contact can be varied, but the preferred low shot will be varied accordingly as a result.

The volley is the hardest shot of all because of the fine judgement needed on angles and the speed at which the ball comes to you. It is essential to get your striking foot behind the line of the ball as it travels through the air, and early body movement to achieve that is essential. As with most shooting, and especially in the case of the volley, the shoulder opposite to your kicking foot should point squarely at the goal – the intended target. If your shoulder is opened up, there is a tendency to drag the ball wide of the far post or slice it past the near post. It is absolutely essential, as with all shots, to keep the ball down and so avoid skying it over the bar, and therefore the ball should be struck on the mid or upper line, with your body leaning over the ball. Your hip and, where possible, your knee

Contact.

Follow-through.

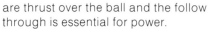

are thrust over the ball and the follow through is essential for power.

Many volleys are performed with both feet off the ground, as with overhead and side-hook volleys. These are very difficult to perform and require a great deal of practice, and it should also be remembered that off-the-ground volleys when performed too close to an opponent can sometimes be penalized as dangerous play.

As stated earlier, all goals are goals, spectacular or otherwise, so that prods off the knee or thighs, toe-punts and chest pushes all count. Good mastery of the ball will allow you to take advantage of a higher percentage of half-chances, where lack of time would otherwise prevent a shot being struck, but the real key is the desire to have a go at goal rather than delay or pass the responsibility – and the ball – to a colleague. Scoring a goal is a tremendously rewarding experience, whether it comes from a dramatic volley or a clumsy toe-punt. Make the most of every opportunity.

RUNNING ·

WITH · & · WITHOUT · THE · BALL

Take a run at it

Soccer coaches now realize that football is an athletic sport and that the best players are good athletes as well as good footballers. Although it is not necessary to be an 'even time' sprinter or a marathon runner to play the game well, you do need to be fit and to run well and efficiently. Running without the ball is a topic in itself, and one which is often neglected. All players should learn to run efficiently, and this requires practice, either in groups or in solo sessions. It is necessary to distinguish the types and amounts of running required for each position on the field. One particular study showed that midfield players ran about 11,000 metres during a game, compared to 8000 for strikers and full backs, 7000 for central defenders and 4000 for goalkeepers. These were averages per game

SOCCER

Shielding (or screening) the ball.

based on several games and included jogging backwards and forwards, sprinting, cruising and even walking.

Too many players run with their bodies all over the place and their arms and legs splayed too far apart. For sprinting, a short stride with powerful, close-to-the-body arm movements should be practised, while for longer stamina runs a comfortable compact shape should be adopted. This 'slimmed down' and balanced running style will therefore help when it comes to actually running with the ball.

Running with the ball encompasses running at angles to players, dribbling with the ball and changing direction, often shielding the ball from opponents at the same time.

Close control of the ball is vital when running with it. The coaching of this skill, normally called dribbling, has varied over the years, from the Stanley Matthews-type running with the ball between the feet to the more sideways approach with the ball on the outside of the foot. Modern players like the Argentinian international Ossie Ardiles are models well worth watching and learning from.

You should learn to run with the ball, keeping it as close as possible and using the outside and top of the foot as contact points. While it is sometimes useful to use the inside of your foot, this can cause problems when trying to get the ball away quickly from an opponent, shielding it at the same time. Sometimes the ball cannot be moved out quickly enough from between your feet, and you will find that there is a tendency to overrun it. Using the front of your foot, the ball is played with your instep along the line that the run is intended to follow, whereas when you use the outside of your foot your body will be to the side of the ball and often closer to it. The pace of your run will be important, so that your opponent can be beaten by sheer pace, a change of pace (acceleration or deceleration) or by deception. In order to achieve any of these

results, it is necessary to have a 'feel' of the ball, which involves learning close control techniques, a 'feathering' touch and an ability to look up while running. Looking up, using the 'split-glance' method, is necessary for spotting your opponents and colleagues alike.

How many contacts are made with the ball during a run will depend on the speed of the run, the running stride or pattern of the runner and the technique employed, but it is essential to be able to shield the ball on the run from an opponent. To do this when the ball is on the outside of one foot, your body weight has to be shifted across the ball so that it is on the side furthest away from the defender. Skilled players on long runs will often demonstrate the art of moving the ball from the outside of one foot to the outside of the other and back again as opponents close in, either to tackle or to force a change of direction. This shifting of body weight to protect the ball is either called by its old name of 'shielding' or the more recent term 'screening'.

The shielding technique is often employed when receiving the ball with an opponent approaching from the side or behind, and the player may have to pivot in order to keep his back between the ball and an approaching opponent, or better still have the opponent to one side, with the ball on the foot furthest away from him.

Deception in dribbling is a skill which has been turned into an art form by some players. Techniques such as feinting to go one way and then going the other way, dragging the foot over the ball or throwing first one foot and then the other over the ball seem to come naturally to some, but most players will need to practise them. In any event, perhaps the most effective technique is to 'clear the space' you intend to dribble into by turning your body sideways on and running across the defender. This has two advantages. First, if he does not follow, you can keep running and thus create an opening; second, if he does follow, his body

weight will be committed in the direction of the run and it will then be possible to check and move back across him into the space he has now left.

Good running is positive running, in the direction of your opponent's goal, and designed to make defenders commit themselves. The advantage is always with the attacker, for he can act, whereas the defender can only react. Since the aim is to throw the defender off balance, deception and close ball control are the attacker's main allies.

WINNING · THE · BALL

Get your tackle in order

Football is a game of opposites, that is, the attacker wants to run with the ball or get into a shooting position, while the defender wants to stop him and hopefully win the ball so that he can initiate an attack for his own team.

To do this, he will either want to win the ball by interception or by tackling the attacker (preferably before he has

Frontal block tackle.

established good control of the ball).

Interception does away with the need for a tackle. It involves anticipating where the ball is going to be played and then getting there first, preferably to gain control of the ball for your side, or at the very least putting it out of play in order to disrupt your opponents' attack. It is therefore necessary to learn how to 'read' the play by watching the opponent with the ball *and* his team-mates. Close marking, either 'touch-tight' or 'shirt-tight' is valuable in this respect, enabling you to stand a good chance of getting to the ball

first when it is played to the player you are marking, but you could even win the ball by leaving a space which invites a pass and then running into that space to cut it off.

If an interception cannot be made, then it may be possible to close down your opponent by tight marking and 'jockeying' him into making an error. Jockeying means turning your body at such an angle to your opponent that you force him to go in the direction you want him to go.

The final method of winning the ball is the full-blooded tackle, either from the front or the side. Tackling from behind is perfectly legal, but not usually advisable because the margin of error is so small that you will be penalized more often than not.

The front tackle is invariably a block tackle, made with the inside of the foot. Timing is vital, especially if the attacker can be caught off balance or does not have full control of the ball. As the tackler, you balance yourself so that your tackling foot can be bought into contact directly through the centre or lower part of the ball. If through the centre, the ball will be blocked, but if you are clever you may, by going through the bottom of the ball, be able to lift it over the attacker's foot and thus create a situation where you can take the ball away or play it off. On making contact with the ball, your ankle must be kept rigid, whilst your non-kicking foot should be placed in a comfortable position to give balance; you should also lean forward and bend your knees slightly, so that the majority of your body weight is behind your tackling leg.

The tackle from the side will either be a block tackle, a prod away, or possibly a block with the heel. Timing here is vital, and either the nearest foot is used as a balance and a pivot to swing the furthest foot round into the ball, creating the block tackle, or the defender will run alongside the attacker and prod the ball away, which is easier to do with the foot furthest away from the opponent.

In the block with the heel, the defender will run alongside and get his nearest leg in front of the ball, blocking it and then stopping and standing as firm as possible. This calls for superb timing, otherwise a foul will be

Tackling from the side.

The slide tackle.

awarded, and the same applies to the sliding tackle, which should always be a last resort because it means going to ground, and the best tackling is always done while standing.

The timing of the sliding tackle and the angle of approach are both vital. The best sliding tackle comes when an opponent has gone past and the defender is going to hook the ball away, either to regain possession, which is pretty difficult, or to play the ball away or into touch. The tackler must aim to get his foot to the ball at the correct pace, so it is necessary to steady the run just before the tackle, to throw out the tackling leg so that the foot is aimed just in front of the ball and then allow both the foot and the body to follow through, with the non-tackling foot tucked comfortably under the body. The best sliding tackles are done with the foot furthest away from the opponent. It is possible to do it with the nearest foot, but an error here will almost certainly allow the attacker to run

clear, or, if he gets a clip on the back of the heels, he will earn a free kick while you get a lecture.

HEADING –

If you want to get ahead, learn to head

However much players are encouraged to play the ball on the ground, it will inevitably be in the air some of the time. Indeed, there is a school of thought which advocates long high passes aimed to drop into danger zones, thus putting defenders under pressure, which might make them mis-head to opponents near to goal. Therefore, the ability to head the ball is a major weapon in the armoury of any footballer. There are two broad categories of heading: defensive heading, aimed at clearing the ball or

starting attacks, and attacking heading, consisting of strikes at goal or passes which create goalscoring opportunities. The 'when, where and how' of the two types of heading are obviously at the opposite ends of the spectrum, but there are some principles common to any type of heading.

Your eyes should focus at all times on the ball, right through until the ball meets your forehead. Your eyes should not shut, even at the point of impact, and your neck muscles should be held rigid, since much of the power in a header comes from those muscles. Extra lift can be achieved by throwing the weight of your body, including your legs, towards the ball. Mostly, players have to jump for the ball, either on their own, or more frequently in competition with an opponent, and a good rule of thumb is to run towards the ball as late as possible but jump as early as possible. This was something which brilliant headers of the ball like Dixie Dean and Tommy Lawton did so well in their opponents' penalty areas, but it is equally useful to defenders.

In defensive heading, the aim is firstly to get in line with the ball, decide where to make contact, time the run accordingly and then make your jump, always ensuring that your eyes are kept firmly on the ball until the point of impact. Most players will use a one-footed take-off, but some prefer two, especially from a static start. The aim is to strike the ball with your forehead at the midline, or preferably the bottom line, thus getting as much height and distance as possible. A good follow-through helps, because the aim is to clear your lines, and you do not want to top the ball or create a knock-down which may give your opponents the chance to score. If you cannot get height and length, go for width, because there is less immediate danger out on the wings. Midfield players follow the principles of

Bobby Charlton scores a dramatic goal for Manchester United against Blackburn Rovers, 1964/5.

defensive or attacking heading depending on circumstances, but since most players come back to cover their own goal at set-pieces these days, it is important for all players to know the principles of defensive heading.

In attacking heading, it is again necessary to get into line with the ball as quickly as possible while it is still in the air, and this will usually mean running into a suitable position. Aim to meet the ball above the mid-line if possible in order to direct it downwards from your forehead, since these type of headers are the most difficult for goalkeepers to deal with. The run and jump should be timed so that you meet the ball at the highest point of your jump, punching through with the head, the neck muscles and as much body weight as you can on to the top half of the ball. If this cannot be achieved because the route to goal is blocked or you are at the wrong angle, aim to head the ball sideways to a colleague, either by nodding it down or flicking it across the goal. To deflect the ball sideways for a team-mate, your neck muscles are used to twist your head just prior to contact so that your forehead directs the ball in the required way. Alternatively, it is possible to make contact with the lower half of the ball and flick your head backwards, thus deflecting the ball to a colleague behind you. This is particularly useful with corner kicks aimed at the near post.

GOALKEEPING

Finders keepers

Whilst the most vital function of a goalkeeper is to be a shot-stopper, that is only part of the story, and if the keeper can catch or gain possession of the ball, the possibilities for attack as well as defence are at least doubled. The goalkeeper is therefore both the last line of defence and the first line of attack.

SOCCER

Catching a cross at the highest possible point.

Without doubt, all good goalkeepers must possess a physical presence, which encompasses agility, flexibility, bravery and speed of action and reaction, all of which come into play at some time during a game. It is a highly specialized position, and training should be geared accordingly. Indeed, so specialized is it that whole books have been dedicated to the art. As with all aspects of football, training and practice are essential, and in particular it is vital to gain mastery of the angles in order to be a great goalkeeper.

There is one feature about the technique of goalkeeping which is often neglected. Just because the goalkeeper uses his hands at every opportunity, regard must still be had for the use of the feet, since they take the goalkeeper into line with the ball, putting him into a position where he can catch the ball

Turning the ball over the bar

Eyes on the ball.

Contact.

Safety, but
eyes still on the ball.

comfortably without having to indulge in unnecessarily spectacular dives. This is most important in developing one of the vital features of the goalkeeper's art – catching the ball, especially from crosses. In English football, the ball is frequently in the air, and because of the strength of strikers in the air, the goalkeeper must beat them to the ball, especially at corners and free kicks. This is a vital part of the goalkeeper's function.

The crossed ball is the most difficult to deal with, and good positioning is vital for the goalkeeper. The further the ball is out on the flank, the further back the goalkeeper should be towards the far post. He can then make a run to catch the ball at the highest possible point before it drops. Since he is able to get his arms and hands up, he will always have the advantage against strikers. Running late and jumping early applies to goalkeepers as well as to headers. It is important to face the cross, keep the ball in view and get into line with it, preferably making the catch while turned towards the ball rather than sideways on to it.

Only goalkeepers with exceptionally large hands are able to catch the ball with one hand, so you must aim to get hold of it with two. The fingers of each hand are spread as widely as possible, with your thumbs kept close together or even overlapped. If it is a powerful cross rather than a lob, your hands must give a little on impact to cushion or take the pace off the ball. It is then necessary to bend your elbows to get the ball down comfortably into the chest, because any little knock while the ball is still held in outstretched hands may cause you to drop it, with disastrous consequences. It is also preferable to take the ball while going forwards into the jump rather than when falling backwards or getting right underneath it.

Sometimes attackers swing the ball inwards just under the crossbar, and here it is often too dangerous to attempt to catch the ball, so you should aim to turn it over the bar. The same principles of body in line with the flight of the ball and eyes on the ball apply, but the palms of the hands and the fingers make contact with the ball at such an angle that the ball is guided or deflected over the bar. One or both hands may be used to tip the ball over.

Punching clear

The one-handed punch.

Punching with both hands.

There may come a time when the ball neither swings inwards to be turned over the bar or round the posts, nor is it catchable because there are too many bodies in the way. Here, you may have to resort to punching the ball away. The things to aim for here are power, height and length, but preferably width, since the ball is less dangerous on the flanks. The further the ball is punched away, the more time the defence will have to regroup. You will follow the same principles as for the high catch, but should keep a clenched fist and try to make a square contact on the middle, or better still bottom part of the ball. A good follow-through is important for power and distance, and although a two-fisted punch is preferable, a good clean one-handed punch will do.

It can be seen that goalkeeping is a position of highs and lows, and the lows come into play when strikers shoot hard and low into the corners of the goal. Wherever possible, the goalkeeper should seek to get two surfaces behind the ball – the first being his hands, and the second his body. If the ball slips through one barrier, the second will be there to save the situation.

A powerful spring is required for diving, with plenty of body thrust, and this in turn helps the extension of the leading arm, with the other arm coming over the top to clamp the ball. Then the ball should be clutched back into the bodyline as quickly as possible. As with all shots, it is vital to decide whether a catch can be made or whether the ball should be deflected around the posts. The worst mistake a goalkeeper can make is simply to parry the ball with either a weak body action or too strong a hand movement which does not cushion the ball on impact. The ball may then rebound into the path of an attacker, whose scoring chances are improved dramatically by the fact that the goalkeeper is stretched out on the ground.

Although the attacker has the initial advantage because he has the ball and is the one who will decide where and how to strike, the goalkeeper can reduce the odds against himself by cutting down the attacker's angles. This is known as narrowing the angle, and is one of the most important things that a goalkeeper must learn.

To understand this concept, it is necessary to realize that when the goalkeeper is on his goal-line he has a large area – about four yards – to either side of him at which the attacker can aim. As the goalkeeper comes off his line towards the attacker, the angle is closed or narrowed, so that the attacker can no longer see such a large target. Eventually, the goalkeeper will reach a point where the target is completely blocked from the attacker's view, thus forcing him to shoot too wide, too high or straight at the goalkeeper. It is important for the goalkeeper to gauge when to come off the line, to come at the right speed, and to do so positively, which means staying on his feet. He will do this by leaning forwards slightly and crouching on his toes, ready to dive either way or move sideways with the attacker. Sometimes the goalkeeper can

Catching the ball in a diving save.

SOCCER

Narrowing the angle

a

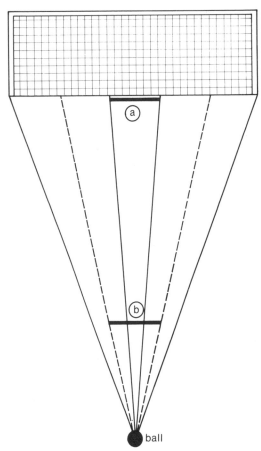

ball

With the goalkeeper in position a, much wider angles are available to the striker than in position b.

force the attacker so wide that his angles are completely ruined.

Closely allied to the principles of narrowing the angle is that of blocking the ball at an opponent's feet. This is more difficult to define, because every goalkeeper has his own style, but it is widely accepted that a front body and hand approach is best, even though some great goalkeepers, like Pat Jennings, used a feet first approach. This can leave you stranded more easily and off-balance, whereas the crouching

Turning the ball round the post in a diving save.

TECHNIQUE

b

Distributing the ball underarm (a, b) or overarm (c).

c

movement is better balanced and the best springboard for a dive at the attacker's feet. If the attacker starts to move round the goalkeeper, the dive should be a sideways one, rather than head-on.

Finally, all good goalkeepers must know how to distribute the ball once they have gained possession of it, thus getting their own team onto the attack. Usually this will involve throwing the ball. A short throw to a team-mate may be just as effective as a long one, and is usually performed with an underarm motion. A long throw is made with an overarm action, rather like a bowler's action or even the sideways action of a javelin thrower. For long throws, your non-throwing arm is thrust forwards in the required direction and your knees bent, while the hand holding the ball is behind the ball, which is then hurled with a powerful body movement and a good follow-through. Of course, you also have the option of kicking the ball, but the overriding consideration is that the receiving player is able to control the ball easily, preferably in enough space to bring it under control before he comes under pressure from the opposition.

Remember – the goalkeeper should be in charge in his own goal area, and preferably in the whole penalty area. He can see virtually the whole of the field in front of him, and should not be afraid to shout advice and encouragement to his team-mates, including demanding the ball from them.

SET · PLAYS · & · RESTARTS

Attacktical approach versus defensive ploys

In considering set plays and restarts, it is necessary to remember that the team which is attacking will be attempting to score, and will take up certain positions designed to further the aim, while the defending side will be taking up countering positions, and each will seek to wrest the initiative from the other. Statistics show that a considerable percentage of all goals come from set plays and restarts, including penalties, free kicks, throw-ins and corners. Other restarts such as goal kicks, kick-offs and dropped balls can be discounted for this purpose.

Many goal-scoring chances come from primary shots or secondary rebounds or knock-downs, so that it is important always to try to get the ball as near to goal as possible if you are not able to score directly. So, for kicks within shooting distance, despite some wonderfully-constructed moves which many coaches work out to get the players to touch the ball around until one gets a clear shot at goal, the best and most likely bet is a direct shot at the goal. Many teams, especially at international level,

The Liverpool goalkeeper Bruce Grobbelaar in full flight.

SOCCER

The dummy run

Player no 4 shapes up to take the kick (a), runs over the ball (b) and leaves the kick to player no 7 (c).

are renowned for this. The Brazilians in particular are experts at scoring with powerful drives or swerved shots from set pieces.

For indirect free kicks within shooting distance, the ball should be played very short to the striker, with possibly another player making a dummy run. It is usually a mistake to play the ball wide to a striker in these circumstances, because although you may want to get the ball wide of the defensive wall, the extra time that it takes the ball to get to the striker may give the defence time to rush him and close him down.

For free kicks awarded a long way from goal, it is still a good idea to get the ball as far forward as possible. It is often useful to try and drop the ball just behind the last line of defence, which may have moved upfield with the idea of keeping attackers away from what would be an offside position. But a well-timed run can take an attacker behind this line and on to a goal-scoring chance without infringing the offside Law.

Considerable possession can be achieved from throw-ins, but teams do not always make the most of them. A long-throw expert in any team is someone to encourage, because he can create chances from unpromising positions. Long throws in the goal area, either with a flat trajectory or a high, teasing flight path can cause all sorts of problems for defenders.

The three major types of corner kicks are those struck high to the far post, those driven or curled in to the near post, and the 'short corner'.

The long kick to the far post requires considerable accuracy, it needs to clear the inevitable ruck of players around the goal area and must reach a player who is capable of heading or volleying for goal as the ball drops. The inswinging corner to the near post has become increasingly popular in recent years because it creates considerable danger, especially if an attacker on the near post is able to flick the ball backwards with his head towards the far post. Colleagues should be aware of the possibilities with these flick-ons from near post corners, and time their runs accordingly.

The short corner is so-called because the ball is simply played to a team-mate standing close to the kicker. There are several variations, but the best is probably to have a receiver standing on the goal-line, because he can then run along the goal-line before pulling the ball back, driving it low in towards the goal or chipping it to the far post area. The receiver cannot be offside because the ball is passed to him along the goal-line, and is therefore not a forward pass.

Whereas attacking from set-pieces can involve individual as well as collective efforts,

good defending at set-pieces is a matter of good team work. Thus, for free kicks at or around striking distance, it is the normal procedure to build a defensive wall. The number of players needed for kicks taken in central positions is greater than is needed for kicks taken from wider points. The goalkeeper must have a clear view, and he should be in charge of lining the wall up. Always put the first 'brick' (player) in line with a post, with another outside that to counteract the swerved shot. After the kick is taken, provided that it has not been simply blasted towards the goal, it is permissible for the wall to rush at the ball, and this should be encouraged.

For longer free kicks, tight marking is essential, so that all attackers are covered, and there should also be provision for picking up any late runners coming round the back of the defence on what is known as a 'blind-side run'. Tight marking is also important in defending throw-ins. Remember – it is easy enough for defenders to give away a goal when they have possession themselves close to their own goal. It is essential to have a man behind the throw for cover if the ball is lost and it is safer to throw the ball up the line rather than square into the field, because a lost ball there could mean a lost goal.

Defending at corners involves the same principles of marking and cover, but it also requires as many players as possible being available to help. The concentration of numbers is no good unless they take up certain basic positions and work with each other – especially with the goalkeeper. The keeper must be the key defender, because it is his job to try to get the ball into his hands. The team defence should always allow the keeper to have both a clear sight of the ball at all times and a clear path to attack the

Kenny Dalglish, player/manager of Liverpool, holds the FA Cup aloft in his greatest moment of triumph, Wembley 1986.

SOCCER

The defensive wall.

ball. This means that he will start out at the back of the goal when the kick is taken and then adjust his position according to the type of kick being attempted. Most frequently, a defender will be placed just inside each of the posts on the goal line. They should not hamper the keeper, and there should be plenty of calling by the keeper, especially if he doubts that he can reach the ball. Sometimes it is possible to threaten the kicker by placing a defender ten yards from the corner flag, thus obstructing the kicker's view of the goal area. This is also helpful when trying to close down a short corner.

The attackers have the advantage at a corner, so defenders must always be alert and flexible. The ideal is for the defenders to gain possession and turn the advantage their way, but clearing the lines is paramount, so powering the ball out of the danger zone must be the priority.

USEFUL
ADDRESSES

FIFA
FIFA House
Hitzigweg 11
CH-8032 Zurich
Switzerland

UEFA
PO Box 16
CH-3000 Berne 15
Switzerland

The Football Association
16 Lancaster Gate
London W2 3LW

The Football League
Lytham St Annes
Lancs FY8 1JG

The Football Association of Ireland
80 Merrion Square South
Dublin 2
Eire

The Irish Football Association
20 Windsor Avenue
Belfast BT9 6EG
Northern Ireland

The Scottish Football Association
6 Park Gardens
Glasgow G3 7YE

The Scottish Football League
188 West Regent Street
Glasgow G2 4RY

The Welsh Football Association
3 Westgate Street
Cardiff
South Glamorgan CF1 1JF

RULES CLINIC

INDEX

One of the game's great 'minds': Osvaldo Ardiles of Tottenham Hotspur.

INDEX